THE WHISPERS SERIES

ABOUT MY BOYFRIEND

Compiled and edited by Kate Johnson

Illustrations by Jim Lefevre and Luke Chaput

Nightingale
An imprint of Wimbledon Publishing Company
LONDON

This book has been written to try and find out how girls really feel about their boyfriends. Not only that, but how do relationships start? How do they grow? And what sustains them?

The quotes provide an honest and intimate look at modern relationships. They are pearls of common wisdom, insights into everyday experiences, and their honesty can help us to understand our emotions better. Too often, important feelings are left bubbling under the surface and people hide their feelings from their loved ones.

This book aims to express the many things that people feel, but often leave unsaid. It's a book of secrets.

Everybody needs to love and be loved. Read it, enjoy it and pass it on.

Kate Johnson
1999

THE MOMENT

'I fell in lust when he took his sunglasses off and I saw his green eyes. I fell in love when we held hands for the first time. Normally any public display of affection makes me uncomfortable and nauseous. But this time was different, it was amazing. I felt protected, loved and adored.'

Sally, 25

'I went home after many years away. At a party, a man came up to me and said, "Hello Teresa." I said, "How do you know my name?" He said, "You were the Angel of the Lord. I've got a picture of you in my wallet." I had been the Angel of the Lord, and he had been a shepherd, at the school nativity play, twenty years ago.'

Teresa, 35

'When we met, he casually brushed a lock of hair behind my ear. I was a bridesmaid at the time and you don't look your most sexy when you're a bridesmaid. It was such a seductive gesture, very intimate, and suddenly I felt ravishing.'

Alex, 27

'I did all the work when we met; it was me that phoned him up. It wouldn't have happened otherwise; he's quite shy, which I didn't know at the time. I decided to take a chance, I knew I wouldn't meet Mr Right sitting in my flat waiting for the phone to ring. It was the first time I've ever liked someone enough to do something about it. Luckily it was also the last.'

Adrienne, 28

'I fell in love with him when I left his house to go to work, and forgot my handbag. I was temping at the time. He realised I didn't have any money on me. That morning, I got a call from reception. He had found out where I was working, I don't know how, and couriered £5 to me.'

Amanda, 25

'I fell in love when I saw him at work. He's a chef. He looked so in charge and professional - very passionate about his job.'

Julie, 29

'We met at a party and I had noticed him immediately. We left the party together to go and get something to eat. If someone had told me then that if I left with him, my whole life would change, I would have said, "I know".'

Valerie, 23

'I fell in love on a long walk with him. When it happened it was a moment of beautiful wisdom.'

Jane, 30

'I fell in love when he lit a cigarette, in the wind, in the car, with the roof down, while he was driving. And then he gave it to me, without me asking.'

Julia, 27

'He had to pursue me - I was testing him. I told him I'd go out with him after four seasons and he thought I was suggesting that we went to a hotel! We've never understood each other since!'

Joanna, 21

'He used to chase me all around the playground. One day I hit him with my tennis racket, and he stopped chasing me. Then I realised that I really liked him chasing me, though I always acted like I didn't. So now I let him chase me.'

Sophie, 10

'I fell in love with him when I was wondering whether to buy some leather trousers. He sent me a list of top ten reasons why I should buy them - number two was that I'd look really sexy, number one was that it would really annoy my mother!'

Kate, 32

'We went out for a drink and he dipped his fingers in a glass, flicked them on my dress, begged forgiveness and asked me to come back to his place so I could get out of my wet clothes. Worked for me!'

Emily, 21

'I fell in love when I saw him revving a jet ski. He looked so carefree, the sun was going down, and I felt excited, like it was a holiday romance, though it wasn't.'

Rachel, 19

'It started with friendship, deliberately. I'd made far too many mistakes based on lust at first sight, so I decided to get to know him, and if we were on the same wavelength, I thought the rest of it would fall into place. He was, and it did.'

Adrienne, 30

'When we started going out it was very casual; a friend had said he was trouble and foolishly I took her word for it. At a Valentine's Day dance he decided to take some bimbo with him instead. I was devastated, but played it cool. The next morning he knocked on my door, I didn't answer, he went away, I cried. Then he came back and played, *You Were Always On My Mnd* by Elvis, very loudly."

Eleanor, 22

'I fell in love with him when I saw him with a child. He was so gentle and kind, and not at all patronising. You just can't fake that - children and animals are innately good judges of character.'

Carol, 29

ROMANCE

'I don't like big romantic gestures, I like very small gestures. I'd rather have the sunglasses, not the trip to Barbados.'

Teresa, 35

'When I was ill in bed, he made me soup, to his own recipe. It was absolutely inedible, and he made me eat it all. Still, I felt like he adored me, because he went out of his way to make me feel better.'

Sera, 35

'I once told him that if I had the money, I'd buy myself an Armani suit. For my birthday, he made a cake with strawberries on the top, each dressed in a little white and brown chocolate Armani suit.'

Sophie, 22

'I know he loves me because he rides for three hours on his motorbike to get to me. In the winter, it gets so cold for him that he has to wear four pairs of trousers!'

Joan, 17

'He's really romantic. He paints my toe nails. Once he took me for a surprise midnight picnic after which he wrote our names on a piece of paper with a burnt match and sent a message in a bottle.'

Georgie, 24

'Romance is being brought a cup of tea in the morning, without having to ask.'

Eva, 27

'Neither of us is romantic, though when he bought some extra towels for me to use at his flat, I realised it was serious. I don't go in for romantic gestures, I don't even bother wearing contact lenses instead of glasses. I try and remember Valentine's day, but I won't do things like wear a negligee...a shell suit maybe! I'm sure he'd understand if I explained I couldn't cook the meal I promised, because there was something good on TV!'

Vanessa, 29

'Once he sneaked home from work to see me, completely out of the blue. We spend a passionate hour together, then he went back to work.'

Claire, 26

'We changed our mobile phones to say 'sweetheart' and 'darling' when we call each other.'

Claudia, 31

'Familiarity is romantic; we were never romantic, so it's never really going to happen. I don't miss it; being yourself and feeling relaxed is romance for me. Doing romantic things is an act - it's what people do to try and impress someone when they start dating. It's not real.'

Judy, 29

Friction

'He likes to get up early, be organised and plan everything, whereas I leave everything to the last minute. I've learnt to let him do it his way, and I ignore it.'

Heidi, 34

'We argue a lot, and always about the same things, especially at the beginning of our relationship. But we've discussed it. We are both very stubborn, and it's been hard for us to compromise, though it gets easier.'

Ann, 24

'I've worked out that we bicker when we're tired, and when we've been out drinking. So when I feel a fight coming on, I force myself to go to sleep instead.

Elise, 33

'It really annoys me when he doesn't turn the windscreen wipers off when it's stopped raining. I used to get sarcastic and say, "Oh, is it still raining?" Now I say, "Would you mind turning them off?" I've become more practical, rather than waiting for him to guess and getting more irritated when he doesn't.'

Vanessa, 29

'He does things that annoy me - like he's really untidy - but they aren't major character flaws. I also had a momentary revelation that maybe I've got faults too!'

Rochelle, 29

'He works long hours, and always very hard. I used to get annoyed if he was late meeting me, or cancelled plans, but I realised that I admire the way that he works hard, and that he's doing it to reach certain goals.'

Vanessa, 29

'I was so busy worrying about giving up my independence, that I didn't realise how nice it was to actually let some independence go. It's not the end of the world to change your plans, and not do the things that you always do.'

Alice, 29

'The hardest part is dealing with his family. They are all very nice to me, but we have had a completely different upbringing. His family comes from before we knew each other and they have a shared history that I'm no part of...It's hard when we criticise our own families, but feel uncomfortable when the other person joins in.'

Jessica, 34

'I made a rule that at least once a week we must have dinner without the TV on. At first, I felt a bit self-conscious, like I was playing at being a grown-up, but it's made a big difference to our relationship.'

Clare, 27

'I'm terrible in arguments, I know all the right buttons to press to annoy him, and sometimes it's very hard not to press them. It takes courage to stay and work out a resolution. Before, I'd sacrifice the relationship to save face and I'd just walk away. But now, the relationship means the world to me, and I would sacrifice anything for it.'

Kirsty, 35

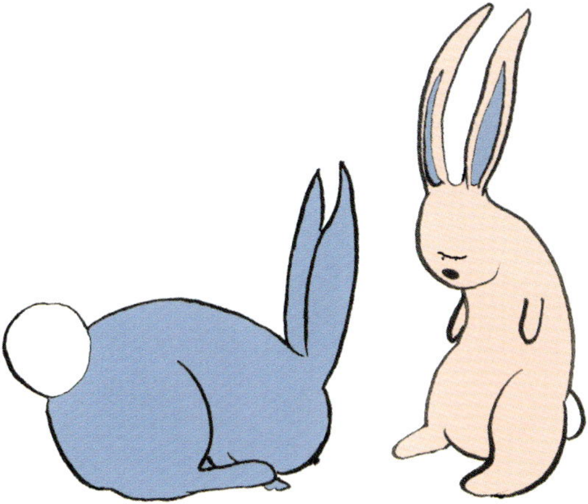

'We made a rule that we don't argue in bed. I don't think it matters if you go to bed without having resolved something either. Things often seem much better in the morning.'

Carol, 29

'I see a quality in his faults. It's ridiculous, when I find that he's been lying - I see it as being creative. Lying has helped him to be very successful in business, but I wish he wouldn't lie to me.'

Teresa, 35

'You can't change anyone, and it's arrogant to want to. Why should they change to fit your whims? I don't think anyone really totally changes, though they can adapt as a result of their experiences. As a rule, so long as it's not a major character flaw, you have to accept it.'

Susannah, 35

'I can forgive but I don't forget. It's a way of ensuring that you don't get caught in the same situation again.'

Alice, 29

'I don't think you necessarily have to really like him; like and love are different, I can separate the two. I wouldn't particularly want to be friends with him, if I wasn't in love with him. And if he was my best friend, it would make me far too dependent on him.'

Laura, 26

'At first, when he did something differently to the way I would do it, I assumed he was doing it wrong. Things like reading the map and planning the trip before we set off somewhere. I'd just drive till I found the place. But I've come to look at myself in a more critical way, rather than trying to find the fault in him all the time. I suppose that's a good thing!'

Veronica, 25

'If problems don't get solved, they get so big they take on a life of their own, and become insurmountable. It's hard to compromise; he looks at things in a completely different way to me. I'm trying to learn that my way isn't always the best or only way all the time...just most of the time.'

Ellie, 28

'It went from casual dating to something serious when we had our first row. He was jealous, and wouldn't admit it. Finally he said he didn't want me to see anyone else. And I didn't.'

Louise, 24

'I haven't really learnt how to compromise, but perhaps the right person is the one who you don't have to compromise for. My relationship is one of mutual respect, so it doesn't feel like a compromise, which I've always resented before. We live separate lives together.'

Emma, 30

'I'm embarrassed how I used to argue. I was a dirty fighter, and I always felt that backing down and apologising was weak. I'm getting better at saying sorry, but very slowly! It's so tempting to say, "I'm sorry, but the thing is...."'

Charlotte, 30

'He was always so non-committal, so I finished it and went away on business. I got a fax saying, "I've bought some new shoes, and I'd like them to see you. Please come back."'

Phillipa, 26

'Compromise only seems to work when he gives in.'

Marcelle, 17

LOVE

'I love him because when it's hot he takes his shoes off and walks around barefoot.'

Emily, 14

'The things that I found annoying about him when I first met him have ended up being things that I love about him, like the way he wears his polo neck jumpers (he doesn't fold the neck over) or his jeans (too tight). It's his general sense of dress, his annoying laugh...it must be love!'

Victoria, 25

'It feels like I'm blue, and he's yellow, and together we can make green.'

Sandra, 15

'I love him when he cuts the grass in his shorts. I like seeing him doing grown up, manly things. I sit back and admire him - and shout out "You missed a bit," just so he doesn't get cocky!'

Carol, 29

'With other boyfriends we'd argue about the same problem, time and time again. I still argue now, but they are different problems, which must mean that we are resolving some of the difficulties. It's a long and slow process to learn to communicate, but it's worth it.'

Sarah, 27

'I don't like it when other girls talk to him a lot. It makes me wonder if he likes them more than me. But if he didn't like me best, he wouldn't walk home with me every day, would he?'

Carole, 9

'I knew I was in love when every second person I saw on the street reminded me of him, and everything that people said reminded me of something he and I had done or talked about.'

Joanne, 19

'I love him because when I'm really tired, he rubs my feet, and strokes my hair until I fall asleep. And he doesn't complain. I tend to make a huge fuss about giving him a back rub.'

Susan, 26

'I fell in love with him when he took me to his parents' home for Easter. It wasn't a big deal for him. He's so honest and up front, it took a long time to get used to it. I'm not honest like that, I play a lot of games.'

Alice, 29

'He's the first boyfriend I've ever had with whom I can walk around naked without feeling self-conscious - in fact I feel the opposite. I don't think about my cellulite, I feel gorgeous!'

Dawn, 24

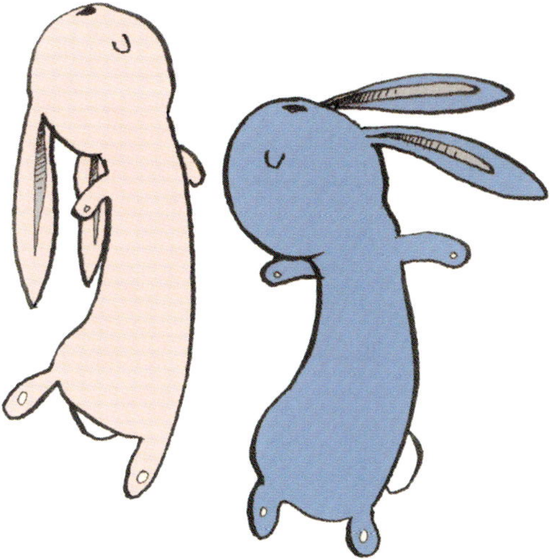

'I love him, but I don't really know why. Life's much better with him in it. It's just a feeling. It's chemistry, I forgive him more than I should, and he probably thinks he does the same for me. To be honest, I think I'd forgive him anything at all. Don't tell him that though.'

Alison, 32

'I can't see the future without him in it. We spent a weekend in Paris togethe. When I said goodbye to him at the airport, I bought a bridal magazine. I couldn't read any of the words, but I looked at the pictures. Scared myself stupid!'

Susie, 21

'One of the best things is that the longer we're together, the more things we share. We've made new friends together, and I want him to think of my friends as his friends too.'

Heidi, 34

'We share the same goals overall. We go about them in a different way - but we want the same things.'

Anna, 29

'I had lots of relationships before this one, and they all seemed to be leading me to him. I went from one extreme to the other - dynamic men, boring men, ugly, kind - all of them, and it feels like now I've got the best bits from all the others in one man.'

Belinda, 26

'I used to have a spotty back, and I'd never let a man see it - but he doesn't mind. It's a big thing to me, but nothing to him.'

Adrienne, 28

'Love is like wearing your favourite comfortable sweater. It just fits.'

Louise, 25

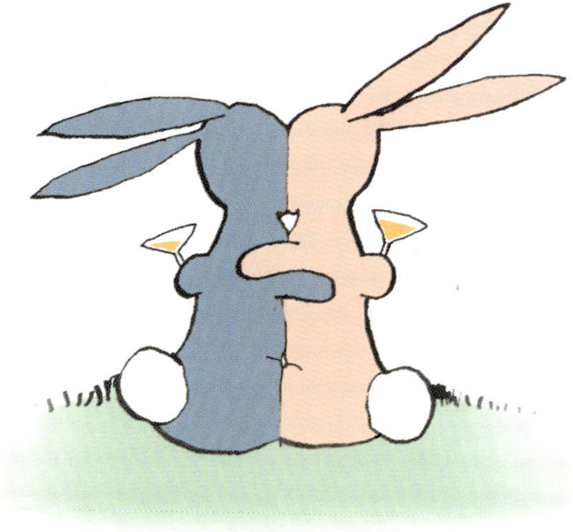

'I knew it was serious when he started planning ahead - not which pub to go to that night but where we'd spend our summer holidays.'

Lauren, 28

'Passion is the ability to get excited about anything, and the ability to make anything exciting. I knew I loved him when I stood in the snow to watch him change the carburettor. It was really exciting!'

Elizabeth, 27

'It's so great to be able to actually go to sleep with him. I'm so relaxed around him that I don't wake up every half hour wondering if I've been snoring or grinding my teeth. At first it felt odd to sleep with him there, and now it feels odd not to sleep with him there.'

Heidi, 34

'It's easy to share the good things with someone, but I love him because he will also share the bad things with me, with very good grace. I can face anything with him.'

Judy, 32

'We have passion for life, with each other, which I never had before. We chased a balloon on the way home together today!'

Susie, 21

'I used to put on make up before I went to bed, and would sneak out in the morning to clean my teeth. But I can kiss him in the morning, even if we've got morning breath - it doesn't matter. I don't even care what I look like.'

Wendy, 28

'I'd forgive anything except infidelity. Maybe I'm being naïve, but I trust him implicitly. If he ever broke that trust, I'd never get it back again.'

Paula, 28

Lessons Learnt

'I used to get upset if I'd been to the doctor or had an interview and he wouldn't ask me about it. I thought he wasn't interested, and we'd argue. But now I've learned to broach the subject myself and tell him what I've done, or what I need from him, and he's always interested and supportive.'

Judy, 25

'It's impossible to be in love all the time. There are always things about him that drive me mad; he often turns up on a date in shorts with a backpack, like he's got another girl stuffed in there for back-up, or he cooks really inedible food or he wears that day's clothes to bed. But then he turns his head a certain way, or he blushes when he sees me and suddenly I'm in love again!'

Donna, 23

'The thing I try to remember is to be very loving. People need to feel loved, and so I try and show love, otherwise it's just friendship plus sex. He knows that I love him, because I show him.'

Ann, 22

'I never used to make an effort in relationships, because I used to think that if it didn't come naturally it wasn't worth it. Now I see that you do have to make an effort, and if you can't, it's not worth it.'

Sally, 28

'When I feel jealous, I tell him, otherwise it spirals out of control. I think he appreciates me telling him, I try and do it calmly, he reassures me, and it doesn't turn into a drama. A little bit of jealousy is a good thing anyway - if I didn't love him, I wouldn't worry about him falling in love with someone else.'

Belinda, 24

'I've always had a fear of being controlled and giving up my independence. Previously, I didn't realise that was happening until it had happened. But I've come to see that giving up a little bit of control can be nice. It's nice when he makes the decisions.'

Judith, 30

'It was a big surprise to find out how difficult it is to compromise. But you have to allow them to be the person you were first attracted to. You can't fit them neatly into your life.'

Lindsey, 30

'You shouldn't spend all your time with that one person, no matter how much you may want to. Life goes on outside relationships. A love should be that magical thing you return to when all the work is done.'

Lucy, 25

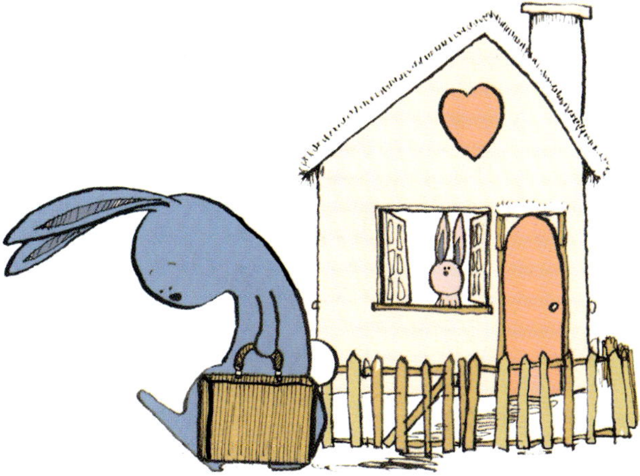

'It's a relief to know that you can have a relationship that isn't all terrible arguments and then passionate making up. This relationship is fun and friendly, and it doesn't feel like I'm missing anything.'

Alice, 29

'Never put on any airs and graces; I'd been kicked in the teeth so many times before, I thought I'd say what I wanted from the beginning. I was lucky that he accepted that, instead of saying goodbye, and that he wants the same things as me.'

Adrienne, 28